15 Reproducible Cut & Paste
Mini-Dictionaries

★ ----------------------------------- ★

Thematic Picture Dictionaries That Help Young Learners Read & Write Lots and Lots of New Words

by M'Liss Brockman and Susan Peteete

SCHOLASTIC
PROFESSIONAL BOOKS

New York • Toronto • London • Auck
Mexico City • New Delhi • Hon

Dedication

We wish to dedicate this book to our family for their support and encouragement and to our students at Goodwin Primary who have helped us refine our picture dictionary throughout the years.

Acknowledgements

Thanks to Sylva Kezar for encouraging us and showing us the way to make our dream a reality.

Thanks to Liza Charlesworth for her editorial insight and suggestions.

Cover design by Josué Castilleja
Cover and interior artwork by Rusty Fletcher
Interior design by Sydney Wright

ISBN: 0-439-26243-7
Copyright © 2001 by M'Liss Brockman and Susan Peteete

Contents

Introduction

Welcome to the wonderful world of mini-dictionaries, where kids make their own fun-to-read reference tools and learn lots and lots of new words.

In this book you'll find 15 reproducible cut-and-paste mini-dictionaries that kids can make and collect. As you're soon to discover, students find making them a fun and easy activity. You may make them as a whole-class activity or as a learning center project. Once kids get the bookmaking process down, you might even send the books home for homework! Their compact size makes them a terrific pocket-reference guide that can be used anytime or anywhere . . . even on the living room sofa!

If you choose to make all of the mini-books before the year is out, your students will have constructed and actively used more than a dozen mini-dictionaries. They'll have learned dozens and dozens of new words, and developed a sense of confidence about the words they're learning to read and write. In fact, your students will have a whole collection of mini-dictionaries they can use as they read and write throughout the year. These dictionaries get students practicing important language skills—and help set kids on the road to reading success.

Sharing What We've Learned

For many years we've been teaching with picture dictionaries in our classrooms. We began using them when our language arts instruction followed a letter-of-the-week-style program. At that time, we asked children to look at objects we had labeled. Each object's name began with the particular letter we were studying that week. Then, we asked students to draw and label each object. Although we were confident our students were learning key concepts of print, the method wasn't meeting our expectations. We wanted our students to make and then use their very own mini-dictionaries as powerful reference tools. The question was, how? After many revisions, we developed the mini-dictionary format we use today. We think you'll love teaching with them. Their fun cut-and-paste format makes them enjoyable for kids to create and easy to use as practical reference tools in the classroom.

We've found that mini-dictionaries are great for teaching early reading, writing, referencing skills, and more. You're sure to discover lots of ways to use these books in your classroom. The list below highlights just a few of ways you may choose to use mini-dictionaries, including . . .

- ✿ Connecting themes with practical hands-on writing and reading activities.
- ✿ Introducing book handling and concepts of print.
- ✿ Improving students' vocabulary in both reading and writing.
- ✿ Putting a powerful reference tool in the hands of young learners.
- ✿ Promoting students' use of phonics skills in meaningful ways.

⚙ Building students' automatic recognition of letters and sounds.

⚙ Strengthening letter-formation skills.

Using Mini-Dictionaries in Your Classroom

Invite your students to use their mini-dictionaries for meaningful learning experiences. Here are just a few teaching ideas to get you started:

✓ Model the use of beginning reference skills by using mini-dictionaries to spell a word correctly during shared writing activities. They are a valuable reference tool in a print-rich classroom, as are word walls, books, lists, and pocket charts.

✓ Encourage students to check their spelling with their personal mini-dictionary. Mini-dictionaries are handy as a reference when writing individual or collaborative class books. Plus, children connect pictures with written words in their writings.

✓ Prompt children to refer to their mini-dictionary entries for inspiration when writing in theme-related journals. On pages 7–10 you'll find some Writing-Prompt Extension Activities to get you started.

✓ Encourage students to use their mini-dictionaries to work independently on reading and writing assignments, which will increase their self-confidence and self-reliance.

✓ Store collections of completed dictionaries in a decorated shoe box or self-closing plastic bag. If you prefer, store them linked together like keys. Just punch a hole through the top left corner of each book in the collection and connect them with yarn, lanyard, or a binder ring.

Assembling the Books

Help your students grow comfortable with making the mini-dictionaries by constructing a few as a whole-class activity. Demonstrate and discuss each of the bookmaking steps—from coloring, cutting, matching words, pasting, and writing, to the actual assembling. After making books together, we've found that our students are eager and able to complete their mini-dictionaries independently.

Tip! For younger students you may want to assemble the books in advance, especially at the beginning of the year. With time they'll become confident bookmakers and delight in making their very own books . . . all by themselves!

Making the Mini-Dictionaries

Creating mini-dictionaries requires few materials and can be done at your students' desks, learning centers, or wherever your students will have easy access to basic supplies. Students will need: scissors, crayons or markers, white glue or paste, and a stapler.

1 Make double-sided copies of the mini-dictionary pages on 8 ½" x 11" paper. Make single-sided copies of the cut-and-paste picture pages on 8 ½" x 11" paper.

2 Have students cut each mini-dictionary page in half along the solid line. Then, ask students to put the pages in order by following these steps:

For an 8-page book, place page 8/1 faceup on top of of page 6/3.

For an 12-page book, place page 12/1 faceup on top of of page 10/3, followed by 8/5.

For an 16-page book, place page 16/1 faceup on top of of page 14/3, followed by 12/5, and page 10/7.

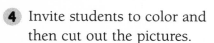

3 Ask students to fold the sets of pages along the dotted lines, making a little book. Have them check to make sure that all of the pages are in sequence. They will then need to staple the pages together along the book's spine.

4 Invite students to color and then cut out the pictures.

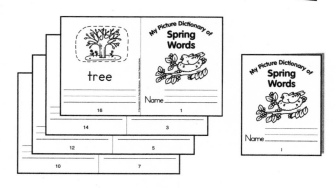

5 Students should then match their pictures with the words in their mini-dictionaries and glue the pictures in place. You may find it helpful to review the process with your students, modeling how one matches the words printed in the mini-dictionaries with the pictures that accompany them. Ask: *What is this a picture of? Where does it belong in our mini-dictionary? What clues do we have about where it belongs?*

6 Once the mini-dictionary is assembled and all the pictures are glued in place, it is time for your students to write the word as it appears on each mini-dictionary page.

Note: During the photocopying process, be careful not to invert any of the double-sided dictionary pages.

> **Tip!** For younger students, consider writing each dictionary word on its corresponding cut-and-paste picture. Then, invite students to match words by examining initial letters, word configurations, and so on.

Writing-Prompt Extension Activities

There are lots of ways to encourage your students to use their mini-dictionaries during the writing process. Copy your favorite writing prompts from the list that follows onto 3" x 5" index cards and tuck the cards in your writing center. Then, ask your students to respond to the writing prompt as part of their center work. Or, if you prefer, select a prompt a day as a journal writing activity. And since mini-dictionaries are so portable, you can have your students tuck the mini-dictionaries you're currently studying in their backpacks with a Writing-Prompt Extension Activity. Linking reading, writing, and referencing skills is easy when you have fun-to-write-about writing prompts like the ones that follow:

School

- Describe the best day you've ever had at school. What happened that made it a special day?
- What subject do you like most in school? Tell three reasons why you like it.
- Write a story about what happened in school today. What happened first? second? third? Write the name of each tool you used in the classroom.

Fall

- Paint a fall picture with watercolor paints. After it dries, write a story about your picture. (Invite younger students to dictate a story while you act as a scribe.)
- If winter never came and it was fall all year round, what would happen to the trees? plants? animals? Write a story called "A Year Without Winter."
- What would it be like to be a leaf in October? Explain your answer. Be sure to refer to several of the items listed in your mini-dictionary.

Zoo Animals

- What is your favorite zoo animal? Write about why it is your favorite animal. Is it a mammal? a bird? Does it have a tail? Be sure to use lots of details.
- Write three animal riddles. Most riddles start with a few clues and then ask the reader to guess the answer. Here is an example: *I have stripes, a tail, and very sharp claws. What am I?* (a tiger)
- Fold a piece of paper in half like a greeting card. Choose one of the animals in your mini-dictionary and find out information about that animal. You may want to take a trip to your school library, interview a member of your family, or take a trip to the zoo. Draw or paste a picture of the animal on the outside of the card and write two or three facts about the animal on the inside.

Weather

- Write about today's weather. Describe what is happening outside your classroom's window and use lots of details. Pretend you're describing the weather to someone from another planet who doesn't have weather like we have here on Earth.
- Fold your paper in half lengthwise, and then in half widthwise. Unfold. You should have four boxes in which to write. In each box write the name of a season. Then, draw a picture and write a sentence about the weather in that season.
- Draw and cut out raindrops, clouds, sun, snowflakes, and other kinds of weather from colored construction paper. Label each type of weather and make a hole at the top with a hole puncher. Then, make a weather mobile by hanging each item from a coat hanger with yarn.

Colors

- Write about your favorite color. Tell why you like the color. Then, list ten things that are that color.
- Make a list of all the colors on a piece of paper. Ask your classmates to tell you their favorite color, then record their answers on your paper. How many of your classmates liked blue the best? red? yellow? green?
- What would happen if everything in the world were the same color? Write the reasons for your answer.

Shapes

- Cut out ten shapes of different sizes from colored construction paper. Then, glue a shape collage on a piece of black paper. On a 3" x 5" card describe your collage, telling about the shapes you used in your design.
- Look around your classroom. What shapes do you see in the objects around you? Make a chart listing objects you see under their shape. For example, in the circle column you might list a clock and ball. In the rectangle column you might list a chalkboard, eraser, or book.
- Write three shape riddles. Most riddles start with a few clues and then ask the reader to guess the answer. Here is an example: *I have no corners and look like a tire. What am I?* (circle)

Winter

- Draw a picture of yourself dressed for a day outside in winter. Label all items in your picture.
- Draw a picture of a snowperson. Describe the steps you took to draw it. What did you draw first? second? third? Explain.
- Describe winter where you live. Is your winter the same as winter at the North Pole? Write about how they are similar or different.

Numbers

- I'm thinking of a number between 6 and 8—what is it? (7) Write a number sentence like this for all of the numbers from one to ten.
- Write a number book with a partner. First, fold five pieces of paper in half. Staple along the fold. Number each page, then draw the correct number of objects on each one. For example, on page 3 show three objects. On page 4 show four objects, and so on.
- Would you rather have six cookies or three chocolate cakes? Explain why.

Opposites

- Work with a partner to write a story using the opposite words in your mini-dictionary. Underline each opposite word in green marker or crayon.
- Illustrate and/or write the words of each of the four pairs of opposites on a separate 3" x 5" card. Then, use your cards to play a favorite classroom game, Concentration. Place all the cards facedown on a desk or table. Invite your partner to flip over two cards in order to match each word with its opposite.
- Would you rather be tall or short? Write a list of three advantages and three disadvantages for each.

Transportation

- If you could visit any place in the world, where would it be? What kind of transportation would you use to get there? Tell why.
- Would you rather be an astronaut or a train conductor? Explain your answer.
- Make a graph that lists all of the ways people can travel. Ask your classmates to tell you how they came to school and record their answers on the graph. How many of your classmates came by car? bus?

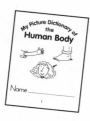

The Human Body

- Trace both of your hands on a piece of construction paper. On each finger write a few words to describe you. List your facial features, hair color, shoe size, and so on.
- Ask a friend to trace your body on a piece of butcher paper. If you prefer, draw a self-portrait using color pencils. Use the words in your mini-dictionary to label your body parts.
- Make a Five Senses Chart. List the body parts you use for each sense. Look through magazines to find pictures that illustrate each sense.

Spring

- Imagine you're a seed that has been planted in soil. What kind of plant will you be? Will you flower? Describe what happens as you grow.
- Imagine you have a friend who has never seen spring before. What should he or she look for as signs that spring is on its way? Illustrate your story.

- Draw a never-before-discovered bird and its unusual nest. Then, give your bird a name. Write five facts you know about your bird on a 3" x 5" card. Attach the card to the bottom of your illustration.

Bugs

- What do you think you could learn from a grasshopper? Imagine you're in a class of grasshopper children. What would you be learning about on the first day of school? the second day? the last day?
- Write a story about your favorite type of bug. Describe and write facts about it. Be sure to include the color, shape, size, number of legs, wings, body parts, etc.
- Many people use pesticides to get rid of bugs in their garden, even though some bugs help our plants grow. Many bugs are food for our backyard animals. Do you think people should use pesticides? Why or why not? Explain.

Farm Animals

- Look at all of the animals in your mini-dictionary. What do you notice that is the same or different about them? Which animals have four legs? two legs? fur? wings? hooves?
- Write a page for a collaborative class book that completes the following sentence: **The farmer saw _____ in the big red barn.** Then, draw a picture that shows what you wrote.
- Make a farm counting book. On each page add one animal. Then, complete the following sentence: **I saw __ (how many) _____ (animals) at the farm.** For instance, your first page may say, "I saw 1 donkey at the farm" and show a picture of a donkey. Your second page may say, "I saw 2 chickens at the farm" and show a picture of two chickens, and so on. Illustrate each page with however many animals you saw at the farm.

Position

- Draw three toys you can find on your school's playground. Beneath each picture, describe how to use the toys. Pretend you're telling someone who has never used that particular piece of playground equipment before. Be sure to use position words in your writing.
- Write a short story using three position words from your mini-dictionary. Your story will need a setting, characters, a problem, and a solution.
- If you could write several new rules for your school's playground, what would they be? Explain why your new rules are fair. Be sure to use five of the position words from your mini-dictionary in your writing.

> **Tip!** For younger students, consider reading the writing prompts aloud. Then to get them started, discuss what steps they'll need to take during the writing process.

Paste
picture
here.

scissors

_____
- - - - - - - - -
_____

16

My Picture Dictionary of
School Words

Name _____

1

15 Reproducible Cut & Paste Mini-Dictionaries   Scholastic Professional Books

---

Paste
picture
here.

pencil

_____
- - - - - - - - -
_____

14

Paste
picture
here.

bus

_____
- - - - - - - - -
_____

3

Paste
picture
here.

book

_____

- - - - - - - - - - -

_____

2

Paste
picture
here.

pocket chart

_____

- - - - - - - - - - -

_____

15

Paste
picture
here.

calendar

_____

- - - - - - - - - - -

_____

4

Paste
picture
here.

paint

_____

- - - - - - - - - - -

_____

13

Paste
picture
here.

marker

_____

- - - - - - - - - - -

_____

12

Paste
picture
here.

clock

_____

- - - - - - - - - - -

_____

5

Paste
picture
here.

glue

_____

- - - - - - - - - - -

_____

10

Paste
picture
here.

crayons

_____

- - - - - - - - - - -

_____

7

13

Paste
picture
here.

computer

_____

- - - - - - - - - - -

_____

6

Paste
picture
here.

lunchbox

_____

- - - - - - - - - - -

_____

11

Paste
picture
here.

desk

_____

- - - - - - - - - - -

_____

8

Paste
picture
here.

flag

_____

- - - - - - - - - - -

_____

9

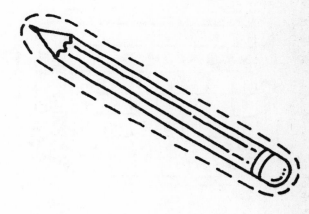

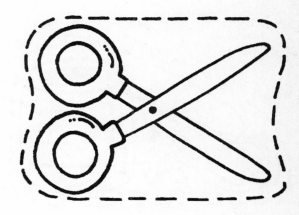

APRIL

	1	2	3	4	5
6	7	8	9	10	11	12
13	14	15	16	17	18	19
20	21	22	23	24	25	26
27	28	29	30			

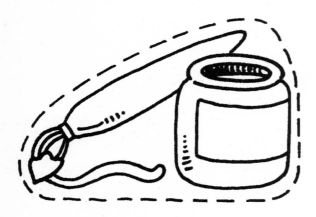

Our Pet Graph

dog
cat
fish
hamster
bird
snake
turtle
rabbit

15 Reproducible Cut & Paste Mini-Dictionaries · Scholastic Professional Books

Paste
picture
here.

rake

16

My Picture Dictionary of
Fall
Words

Name

1

15 Reproducible Cut & Paste Mini-Dictionaries   Scholastic Professional Books

Paste
picture
here.

tractor

14

Paste
picture
here.

apples

3

Paste
picture
here.

Paste
picture
here.

acorn

vegetables

2

15

Paste
picture
here.

Paste
picture
here.

barn

squirrel

4

13

Paste
picture
here.

scarecrow

_____

- - - - - - - - - - - - - - - - - -

_____

12

Paste
picture
here.

corn

_____

- - - - - - - - - - - - - - - - - -

_____

5

Paste
picture
here.

leaves

_____

- - - - - - - - - - - - - - - - - -

_____

10

Paste
picture
here.

fire engine

_____

- - - - - - - - - - - - - - - - - -

_____

7

Paste
picture
here.

farmer

6

Paste
picture
here.

pumpkins

11

Paste
picture
here.

fire fighter

8

Paste
picture
here.

hay

9

Paste
picture
here.

zebra

_____

16

15 Reproducible Cut & Paste Mini-Dictionaries   Scholastic Professional Books

My Picture Dictionary of
Zoo Animals

Name _____

1

Paste
picture
here.

snake

_____

14

Paste
picture
here.

bear

_____

3

Paste
picture
here.

alligator

2

Paste
picture
here.

tiger

15

Paste
picture
here.

camel

4

Paste
picture
here.

seal

13

Paste
picture
here.

rhinoceros

_____

_____

12

Paste
picture
here.

elephant

_____

_____

5

Paste
picture
here.

kangaroo

_____

_____

10

Paste
picture
here.

giraffe

_____

_____

7

flamingo

_____
- - - - - - - - - - -
_____

6

monkey

_____
- - - - - - - - - - -
_____

11

gorilla

_____
- - - - - - - - - - -
_____

8

hippopotamus

_____
- - - - - - - - - - -
_____

9

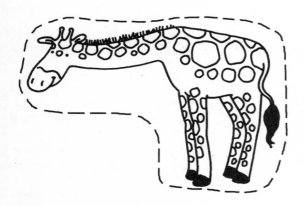

Paste
picture
here.

windy

8

My Picture Dictionary of
Weather Words

Name

1

15 Reproducible Cut & Paste Mini-Dictionaries   Scholastic Professional Books

---

Paste
picture
here.

snow

6

Paste
picture
here.

foggy

3

Paste
picture
here.

cloudy

2

Paste
picture
here.

sunny

7

Paste
picture
here.

lightning

4

Paste
picture
here.

rain

5

Paste
picture
here.

yellow

12

15 Reproducible Cut & Paste Mini-Dictionaries   Scholastic Professional Books

My Picture Dictionary of
Color
Words

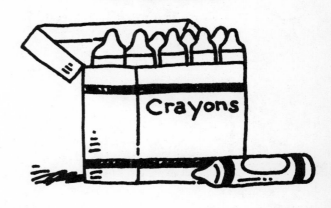

Crayons

Name

1

Paste
picture
here.

red

Paste
picture
here.

blue

10

3

Paste
picture
here.

black

2

Paste
picture
here.

white

11

Paste
picture
here.

brown

4

Paste
picture
here.

purple

9

green

orange

6

7

pink

gray

8

5

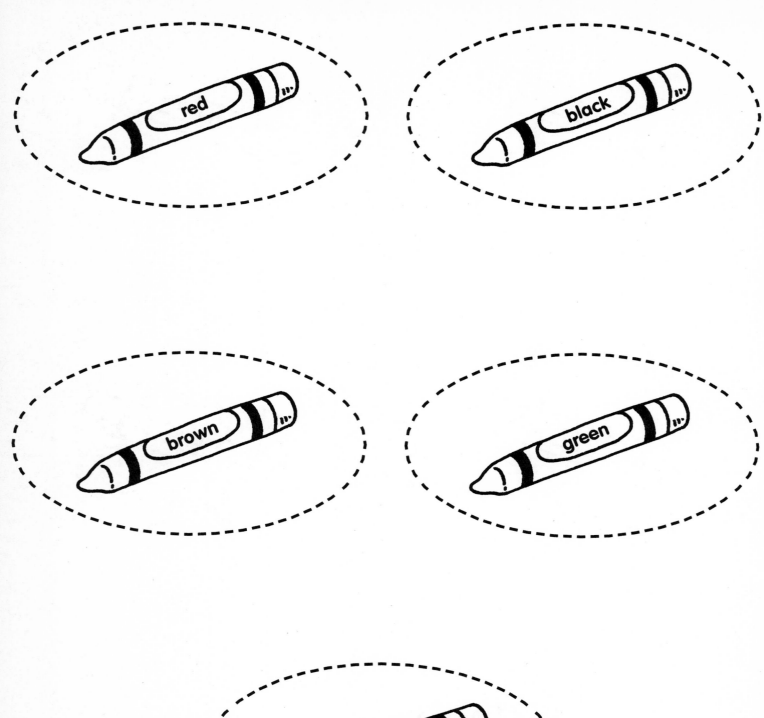

15 Reproducible Cut & Paste Mini-Dictionaries   Scholastic Professional Books

Paste
picture
here.

triangle

_____

- - - - - - - - - - - - -

_____

8

15 Reproducible Cut & Paste Mini-Dictionaries   Scholastic Professional Books

My Picture Dictionary of
Shape
Words

Name _____

1

Paste
picture
here.

rectangle

_____

- - - - - - - - - - - - -

_____

6

Paste
picture
here.

diamond

_____

- - - - - - - - - - - - -

_____

3

circle

2

square

7

hexagon

4

oval

5

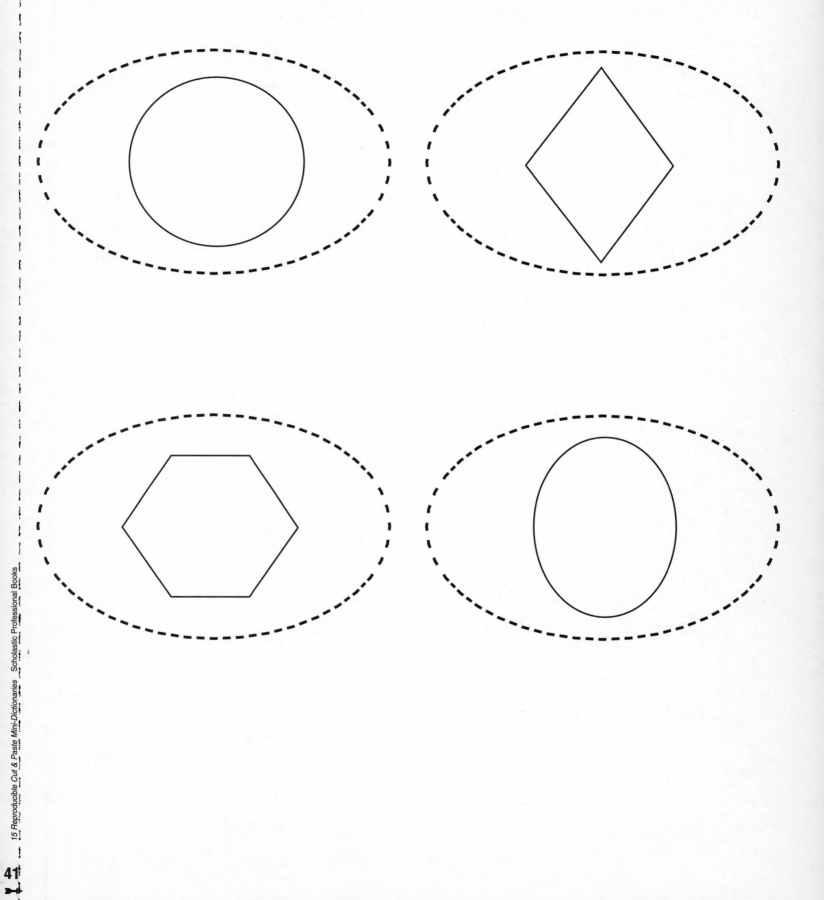

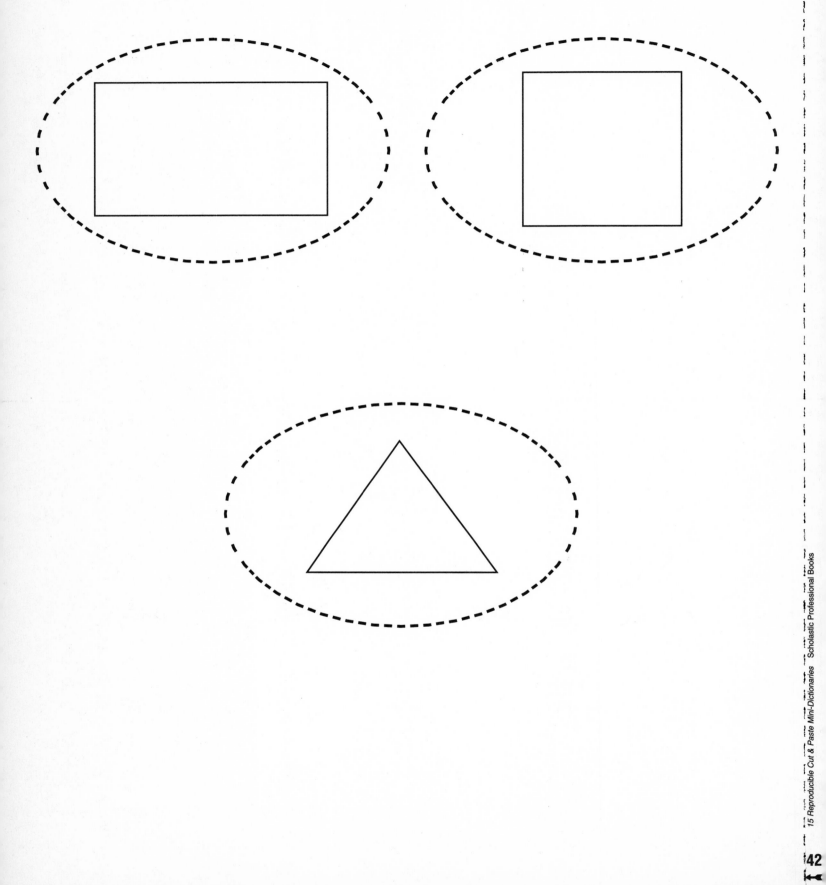

Paste picture here.

snowmobile

_____

16

My Picture Dictionary of
Winter Words

Name _____

1

Paste picture here.

snowflake

_____

14

Paste picture here.

cap

_____

3

boots

2

snowman

15

earmuffs

4

sled

13

44

skiing

fireplace

12

5

mittens

ice skates

45

10

7

Paste
picture
here.

hibernating

6

Paste
picture
here.

scarf

11

Paste
picture
here.

icicles

8

Paste
picture
here.

jacket

9

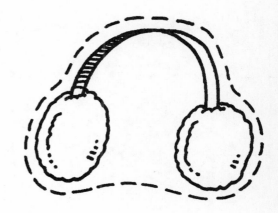

Paste
picture
here.

ten

_____

- - - - - - - - - - - - - - - - - -

_____

12

15 Reproducible Cut & Paste Mini-Dictionaries   Scholastic Professional Books

My Picture Dictionary of
Number Words

Name _____

1

Paste
picture
here.

eight

_____

- - - - - - - - - - - - - - - - - -

_____

10

Paste
picture
here.

one

_____

- - - - - - - - - - - - - - - - - -

_____

3

zero

2

nine

11

two

4

seven

9

four

five

6

7

six

three

8

5

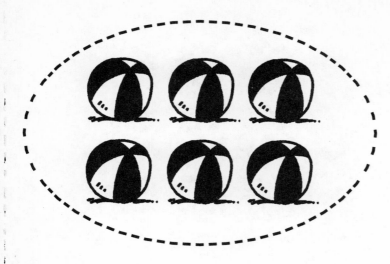

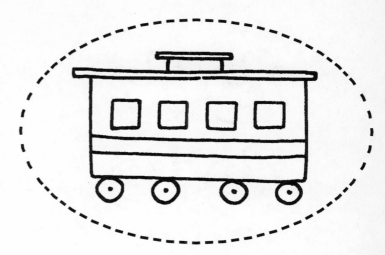

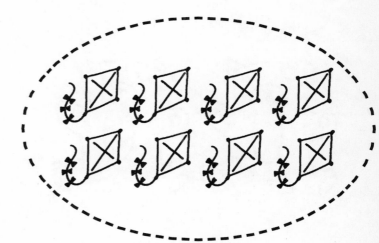

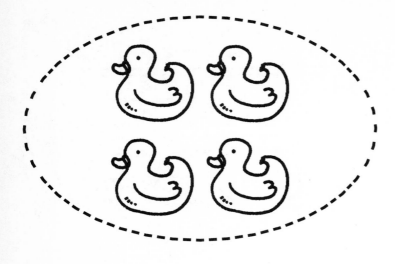

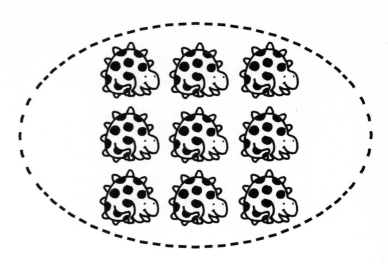

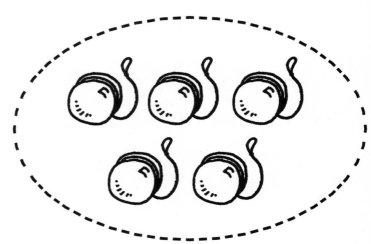

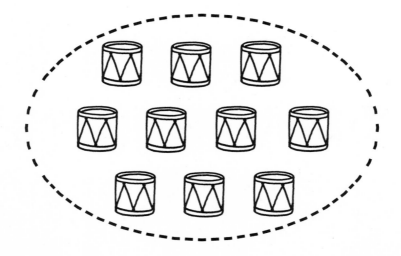

My Picture Dictionary of
Opposite Words

15 Reproducible Cut & Paste Mini-Dictionaries   Scholastic Professional Books

Name _____

1

Paste
picture
here.

short

_____

14

Paste
picture
here.

little

_____

3

big

- - - - - - - - - - - - - - - - - - -

2

long

- - - - - - - - - - - - - - - - - - -

15

open

- - - - - - - - - - - - - - - - - - -

4

near

- - - - - - - - - - - - - - - - - - -

13

Paste
picture
here.

far

12

Paste
picture
here.

close

5

Paste
picture
here.

heavy

10

Paste
picture
here.

cold

7

hot

6

light

11

wet

8

dry

9

Paste
picture
here.

walking
_____

16

15 Reproducible Cut & Paste Mini-Dictionaries   Scholastic Professional Books

My Picture Dictionary of
Transportation
Words

Name _____

1

Paste
picture
here.

train
_____

14

Paste
picture
here.

bicycle
_____

3

Paste picture here.

airplane

2

Paste picture here.

truck

15

Paste picture here.

bus

4

Paste picture here.

taxi

13

space shuttle

_____

- - - - - - - - - - - - -

_____

12

canoe

_____

- - - - - - - - - - - - -

_____

5

sailboat

_____

- - - - - - - - - - - - -

_____

10

helicopter

_____

- - - - - - - - - - - - -

_____

7

Paste
picture
here.

car

6

Paste
picture
here.

ship

11

Paste
picture
here.

hot-air balloon

8

Paste
picture
here.

motorcycle

9

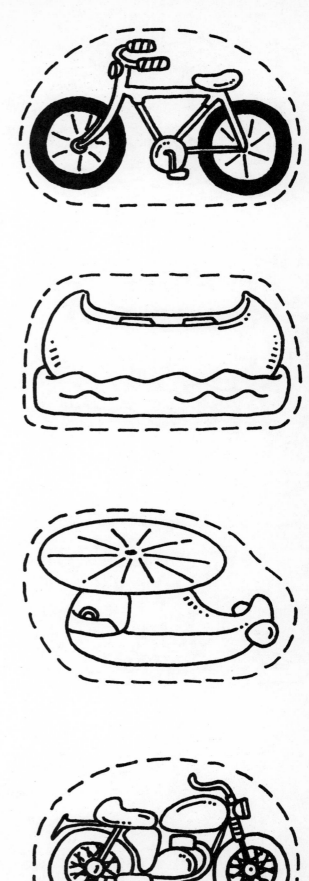

Paste
picture
here.

shoulder

_____

16

15 Reproducible Cut & Paste Mini-Dictionaries   Scholastic Professional Books

My Picture Dictionary of
the
Human Body

Name _____

1

Paste
picture
here.

neck

_____

14

Paste
picture
here.

ear

_____

3

arm

2

nose

15

elbow

4

mouth

13

leg

12

eyes

5

head

10

foot

7

fingers

6

knees

11

hair

8

hand

9

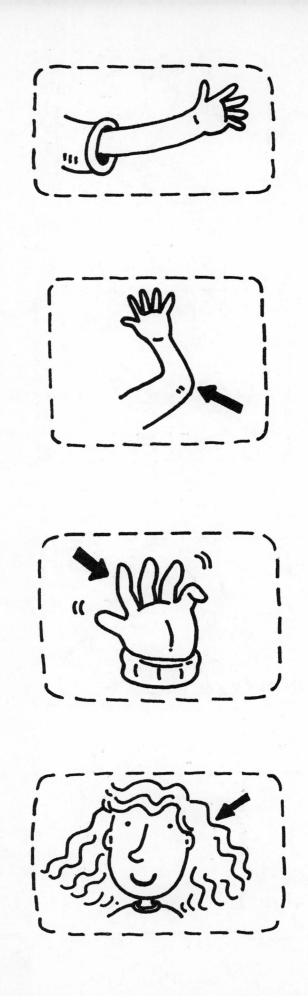

Paste
picture
here.

tree

16

15 Reproducible Cut & Paste Mini-Dictionaries   Scholastic Professional Books

My Picture Dictionary of
Spring
Words

Name

1

Paste
picture
here.

soil

14

Paste
picture
here.

buds

3

birds

_____

- - - - - - - - - - -

_____

2

stem

_____

- - - - - - - - - - -

_____

15

eggs

_____

- - - - - - - - - - -

4

shovel

_____

- - - - - - - - - - -

_____

13

Paste
picture
here.

seeds

12

Paste
picture
here.

flower

5

Paste
picture
here.

rake

10

Paste
picture
here.

leaves

7

Paste
picture
here.

hoe

_____

- - - - - - - - - - -

_____

6

Paste
picture
here.

roots

_____

- - - - - - - - - - -

_____

11

Paste
picture
here.

nest

_____

- - - - - - - - - - -

_____

8

Paste
picture
here.

plants

_____

- - - - - - - - - - -

_____

9

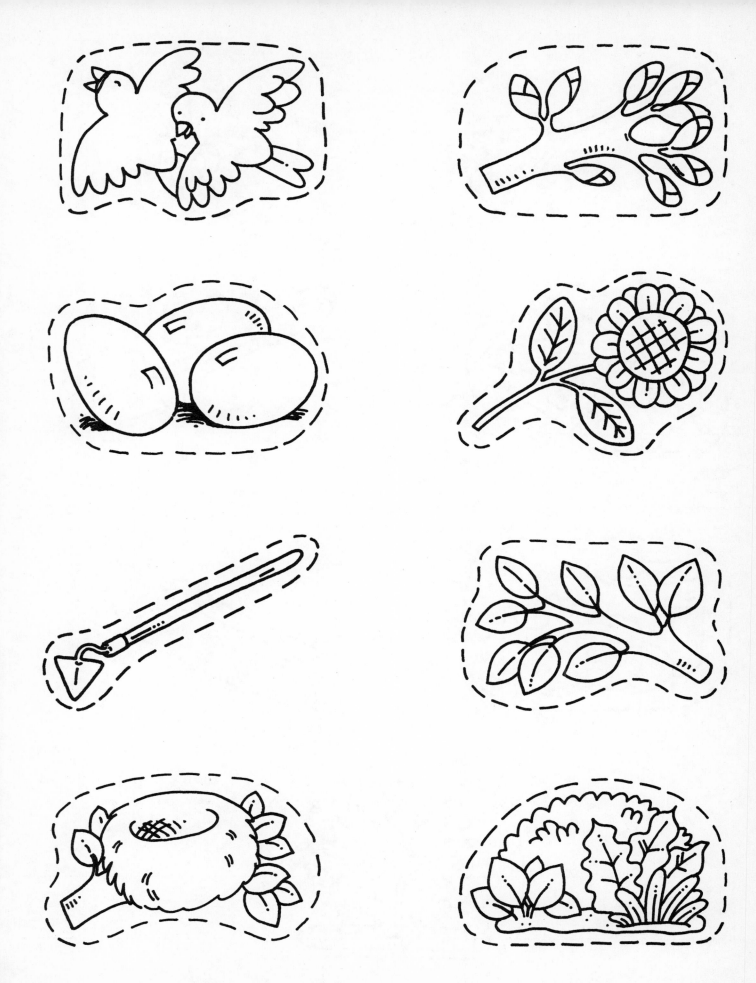

Paste
picture
here.

worm

_____

- - - - - - - - - - - - -

_____

16

My Picture Dictionary of
Bugs

_____

Name _____

1

Paste
picture
here.

spider

_____

- - - - - - - - - - - - -

_____

14

Paste
picture
here.

bee

_____

- - - - - - - - - - - - -

_____

3

15 Reproducible Cut & Paste Mini-Dictionaries   Scholastic Professional Books

79

ant

2

walking stick

15

butterfly

4

snail

13

roach

12

caterpillar

5

mosquito

10

fly

7

Paste
picture
here.

firefly

6

Paste
picture
here.

praying mantis

11

Paste
picture
here.

grasshopper

8

Paste
picture
here.

ladybug

9

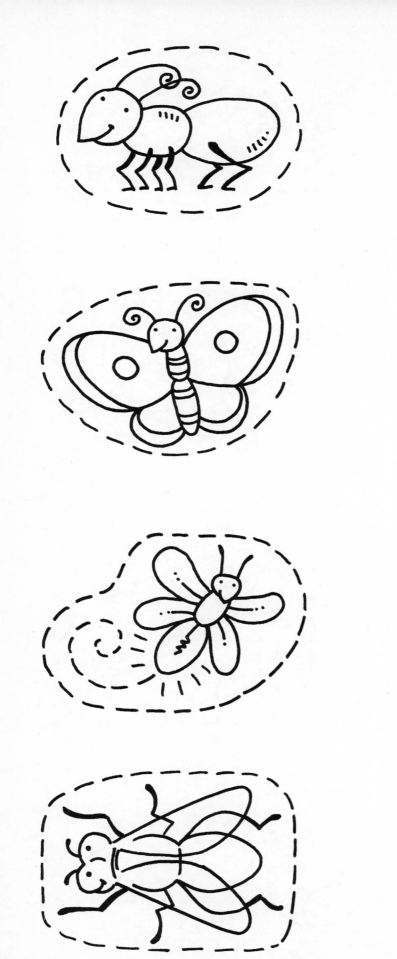
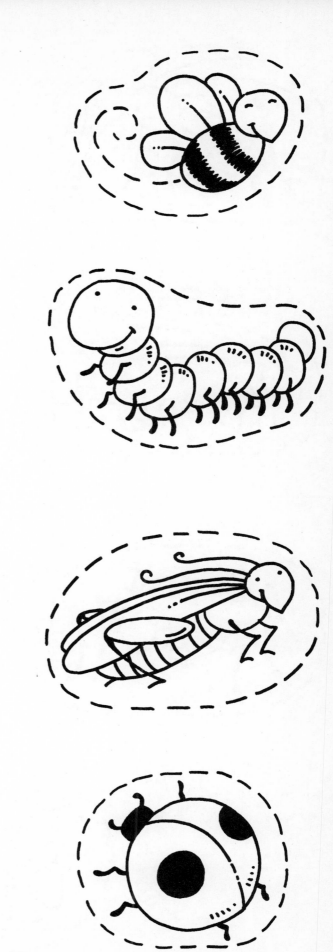

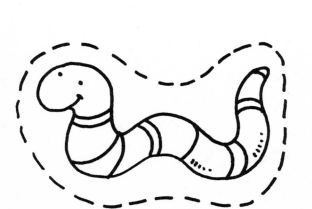

Paste
picture
here.

turkey

16

15 Reproducible Cut & Paste Mini-Dictionaries   Scholastic Professional Books

My Picture Dictionary of
Farm
Animals

Name

1

Paste
picture
here.

rooster

14

Paste
picture
here.

chick

3

Paste
picture
here.

cat

_____

- - - - - - - - - - - - - -

_____

2

Paste
picture
here.

sheep

_____

- - - - - - - - - - - - - -

_____

15

Paste
picture
here.

cow

_____

- - - - - - - - - - - - - -

_____

4

Paste
picture
here.

rabbit

_____

- - - - - - - - - - - - - -

_____

13

Paste
picture
here.

Paste
picture
here.

pig

dog

12

5

Paste
picture
here.

Paste
picture
here.

horse

goat

10

7

Paste
picture
here.

duck

_____

- - - - - - - - - - - - -

_____

6

Paste
picture
here.

lamb

_____

- - - - - - - - - - - - -

_____

11

Paste
picture
here.

goose

_____

- - - - - - - - - - - - -

_____

8

Paste
picture
here.

hen

_____

- - - - - - - - - - - - -

_____

9

Paste
picture
here.

last

_____

16

15 Reproducible Cut & Paste Mini-Dictionaries   Scholastic Professional Books

My Picture Dictionary of
Position
Words

Name _____

1

Paste
picture
here.

first

_____

14

Paste
picture
here.

under

_____

3

over

2

middle

15

on

4

right

13

left

12

off

5

far

10

out

7

Paste
picture
here.

in

6

Paste
picture
here.

near

11

Paste
picture
here.

up

8

Paste
picture
here.

down

9